GOD'S ANSWER
TO LIFE STRUGGLES

Kenneth E. Piper

Publishing in the United States of America
Publisher: Luminous Publishing
www.luminouspublishing.com

For bulk orders or other inquiries, email:
info@luminouspublishing.com

TABLE OF CONTENTS

"It is good for me that I have been afflicted,
That I may learn Your statutes."

Psalm 119:71 (NKJV)

DEDICATION

Life has its own way of introducing itself. Sometimes it's through pleasure and happiness. Other times, it's through challenges and regret. Regardless of how the introduction is made, life will say, "Hello."

I would like to dedicate this body of work to everyone and everything that has served in my life introducing itself to me, resulting in my getting to know Jesus Christ.

For every heart break, I say "Thank you."

For every triumph, I say "Thank you."

To every person who has loved me in spite of me, I say "Thank you."

To every person who has made an occupation out of dragging me down, I say "Thank you" as well.

The entire journey has fueled the passion that burns inside of me to share how God has used it all for His glory.

Looking back only captures where I was. Embracing the present only reminds me of the beauty of now. Looking forward takes my breath away! People will still do what they do. Situations will continue to arise. All of that is good news. I can't wait to see how God will use that new material. So, life, don't stop. God and I...we're steady as a rock.

INTRODUCTION

Before the beginning of time, God had people and promise on His mind. He was so excited that He joined forces with every aspect of Himself to create mankind. The Bible records Him saying, "Let Us make man in Our image, according to Our likeness."

He created man and gave them dominion over the earth and called it very good. God's initial plan, although it was the best for everyone, was challenged when Adam committed high treason in the Garden of Eden. That marked the beginning of struggle through selfishness and disobedience. From that point on, every human being was born with a genetic deposit from the first man, Adam. That deposit is a sinful nature—a propensity to do wrong, and in most cases, enjoy it along the way.

Everyone is born with a blood source that goes all the way back to Adam. We arrived here in need of divine help. We arrived here in need of a total blood transfusion. We were in need of life because we were born into death. The Bible says Jesus is the way, the truth, and the life. Therefore, without Him, we are the walking dead.

It is pretty reasonable to accept that anyone who is walking around dead on the inside will struggle on the outside. Life without Jesus amounts to life with the devil. The only one who has conquered the devil and made a spectacle of him and his work is Jesus Christ. He, and He alone, is your answer to the struggles of life. Satan is the root cause of all struggles. Jesus has already defeated him. He knows everything about him because He created him.

In Christ, there is no victory without struggle. There is no elevation without tribulation. There will be trials and tribulation until the end of time, and God will use it all for His glory. God has provided the answer to all of the challenges of life.

As you read through this book, find yourself and apply what is revealed. Within this spiritual buffet, God has provided meals and medicine for everyone. The question is, are you hungry? Are you sick? Are you tired of being conquered by satan and his plethora of lies and empty promises? Allow God to guide you from hardship to relationship, a relationship that will forever prepare you for all that satan can and will conjure up. Satan will continuously present opportunities to wreak havoc in your life.

With Jesus Christ being your savior and lord, no weapon formed against you shall prosper. The battles of life are not yours. They're the Lord's! And can I share some good news with you? They're already won!

Allow the words in this book to minister to your area of need. Apply this food and medicine where it is needed in your life. Regardless of your situation, God has the solution. There is no earthly problem or dilemma that heaven has not already addressed. Allow God to step right in the center of your situation. Now, brace yourself for transformation. I encourage you to prepare as best you can. You are about to experience the power of that man named Jesus. Your struggles will not stand a chance. I am confident because He did it for me. He will do the same for you. Let's take this journey.

Kenneth E. Piper

HOPE

A colored slip of paper with your name on it, signifies your last day on the job.
After twenty-five years of dedicated service, you feel you've been robbed.
As you process out and prepare for the unknown,
although you have hope, your attitude is blown.

A trip to the doctor for a routine medical exam,
reveals a diagnosis not covered by your medical plan.
The cost is horrendous and the prognosis is bleak.
You begin to wonder, "Can hope even compete?"

Your child calls you from the police station.
You thought they were in school,
not somewhere indulging in married folk sensations.
Hope says, "Don't give up."
Your mind says, "I've had enough."
Hope says, "All this is part of a bigger plan."
Your mind says, "Going forward? I don't think I can."

As this battle continues, and mental blows are thrown,
hope is the victor because of Jesus Christ's work on the throne.
Hope is the younger brother of faith in a fight.
When life gets rough, keep that clearly in sight.

In this world, times will get tough,
but God's solution is more than enough.
As you embrace hope and hold hands with faith,
face all of life's troubles under the umbrella of God's Grace.
He died so you could receive all that you believe.
Believe in His plan. He says, "You can."
The devil is a liar; his tactics are an illusion.
You don't believe me? Just read your Bible for the final conclusion.

REAL HELP

✝

FIRST	THEN
Romans 3:23	1 Peter 5:10
Romans 6:23	Psalm 130:5
Romans 5:8	Romans 8:24
Romans 10:9	Hebrews 11:1
Romans 10:13	John 16:33
Romans 5:1	
Romans 8:1	

FACES

As I look into the closet that is safely tucked away in my mind,
based on the circumstances, which face will it be this time?
Although I am sad, I choose to smile.
Although it's funny, I choose to frown.

With the face of truth knocking on the door of my heart,
I disregard it and tell truth, "Please don't start."

God assures you that truth shall set you free.
Regardless of the circumstances, believe you me!
When this world dictates which face you choose, the devil is the winner.
Checkmate, you lose.

In God's system, one face fits all.
The face of Jesus is universal.
For a confirmation, just ask Apostle Paul.
His transformation from Saul to Paul qualifies him to answer that call.

For every situation, the devil has a face.
He will fool you and trick you until you leave this place.
Situations can change and they often will.
Love is Jesus' face; check the cross. It speaks, still.

With love as your face,
it will clearly replace
every other face
in your closet space.
Regardless of the situation, handle it in love.
It's God's responsibility when seen from above.
Choices and faces go hand in hand.
You only need one face—Love—God's master plan.

Real Help

✝

FIRST	THEN
Romans 3:23	John 13:35
Romans 6:23	Romans 12:1-2
Romans 5:8	
Romans 10:9	
Romans 10:13	
Romans 5:1	
Romans 8:1	

HIDDEN TREASURE

✝

Am I really more than what the eye can see?
That really depends on who is looking at me.
I have been called everything from a genius to a fool.
How can that be said and it all be true?

People have a way of labeling your life.
They seem to think that truth is locked and secured in their sight.
How can faulty eyes judge a faulty life right?
Explain how those same eyes can see spiritual light.

When I have accepted Jesus Christ and received a new life,
it sometimes takes a little time to see, what has happened to me.
Based on experience of the previous me,
you decided long ago that was all I would ever be.

That is really a shame. I have some news.
That person is dead. God paid my dues.
When I gave Him my death, He gave me His life.
He took all of my wrongs and made everything right.

So, stop looking on the surface for what's of real value.
My treasure is His Spirit, hidden within to compel you.
Compel you to seek the true riches of life,
riches like love, peace, hope, and insight.

To receive all that would surely be enough,
but we are talking about God who created us from dust.
When you invite Him in and surrender to His will,
He now has a body to transport His skills.

Supernatural things begin to happen everywhere you go,
things like miracles and healings, just because you say so.
With this type of stuff going on, news travels quick.
People begin to comment as if it were all tricks.

All the excitement and talk changed when they saw who it was.
It had to be God creating such a buzz.
They thought that statement would be insulting to me,
but again, they were wrong. It was God. We agree.

I forgive those who think and act the way they do.
They can't help themselves. I was that way too.
It will never matter, regarding people's feelings about what they see.
When it pertains to me, my true value rests in who lives in me.
So, don't ever think for a minute that you are stuck without hope or a chance.
God is waiting for your "Yes," so He can take a stance.
The treasure in you was fully paid for from the beginning.
Accept it now, and change losing to winning.

Only God knows your true value and worth.
He labeled you priceless before you ever entered earth.
Ignore what you hear if it contradicts that fact.
God's word settles it. That's the end of that!

Real Help

✞

FIRST	THEN
Romans 3:23	2 Corinthians 4:7-9
Romans 6:23	2 Corinthians 5:17
Romans 5:8	Galatians 2:20
Romans 10:9	
Romans 10:13	
Romans 5:1	
Romans 8:1	

IN THE SONSHINE

✝

How wonderful it is to rest in His peace;
a confident assurance in everything He sees,
a life filled with opportunities to grow,
growth often comes masked as challenge, you know.

You were forewarned of this from the very beginning.
The product of disobedience that resulted in sinning.
Growth is a process that results in a debt,
but it's paid in full. No need to fret.

Basking in the SONshine of a carefully planned life,
every step ordered, He's won your fight.
When you receive a bad report or a costly summons to report to court,
remember who's in charge and command anxiety to abort.

Allow the SON to continue to shine.
Remember His promises and be reminded, you're fine.
Someone you love stepped out of your life?
A knock on your heart's door—You answer. It's strife.

The SON continues to shine, regardless of the situation.
God knows trouble never takes a vacation.
His love rays of brilliance freeze bad in its place,
transforming its result into a brand new case.

That little bit of bad was the final ingredient needed.
To showcase God's glory and display satan defeated.
So, let the SON shine and reveal you're fine.
The devil loses again, incapable of amends.

Now put on your SONglasses and enjoy the view.
Life will have challenges, but God's word is true.
He made a promise to never leave or forsake you.

That promise alone is bold and strong.
It's enough to carry you from earth, all the way to your heavenly home.

God's statement, "The Son always shines on those who are mine,"
securely planted in your conscious, will work every time.

Relax. You're fine.
God says again, "Relax. You're mine."

Real Help

✟

FIRST	THEN
Romans 3:23	John 8:12
Romans 6:23	John 1:1-4
Romans 5:8	1 John 1:5
Romans 10:9	2 Timothy 3:16
Romans 10:13	Psalm 119:151
Romans 5:1	
Romans 8:1	

DON'T BELIEVE THE HYPE

The labor pains are closer. The moment is nearing.
The sweat is pouring. The head is appearing.

What started months ago, is coming to fruition.
It's a brand new life, a fresh new addition.

Satan is overjoyed to start this mission.
With eternal failure the goal, satan is always eager to play his role.

The child is immediately assigned a demonic influence
because Momma is lost and oblivious to it.

As the child begins to grow, teaching them the word "No,"
is like telling STOP to GO and calling a friend a foe.

You think your voice is their only direction.
Think deeper, my friend. There's an insurrection.

You try your best to teach what's right.
Your best is not sufficient to compete in this fight.

Do not believe what you see, because it's really just hype.
What is actually going on requires spiritual sight.

Everyone is being counseled by unseen advice.
Evaluate your thoughts and take a look at your life.
That's a great indication of who is refereeing your fight.
If you are living in this world and everything is grand,
supporting selfishness and "getting all you can,"
that's demonic influence working in man,
not realizing you support the devil's plan.

One summer day, you're just having a little fun,
playing bad while carrying a gun.

Tempers arise for no real reason.
You remember you're strapped, and now it's open season.

When it's all done and the smoke clears,
fifteen to life precede those tears.

How can this be? I made a mistake.
No, this was planned through a demonic blind date.
You think your battle is with what you see.
The truth is, what you see comes from what is unseen.
Don't believe the hype. You are on the wrong team.

Continuing this course will only get worse.
The devil's alive orchestrating a curse.

You are not trapped without a solution.
There is a remedy for heartache and confusion.

All answers rest in the wisdom of God,
a gift from above, acceptance is not hard.

Bow your head and accept God's son.
The battle is over. It's already won.

Truth has arrived. Hype is gone.
The devil is defeated, now heaven's your home.

Challenges will come. They often do.
Remember whose blood is all over you.
Just remember whose blood is all over you.

Real Help
✟

FIRST	THEN
Romans 3:23	Galatians 6:7-8
Romans 6:23	Romans 12:2
Romans 5:8	John 8:44
Romans 10:9	1 Peter 5:8
Romans 10:13	
Romans 5:1	
Romans 8:1	

HURT SHOWED ME

Here we go. It's a new day.
Same old headache. My life's a fake.

My children are grown. I know they are happy.
I did my best. They labeled it crappy.

I go to work every day, filled with zest,
whether it's a good day or an outright mess.

I continue to pray for change to come.
I look up toward heaven, where my help comes from.

I attempt to explain something said in the heat of the moment.
Now I dread what was heard because now I have to own it.

I try to make clear that my primary intention,
was not to cause pain but to address the dissention.

It really doesn't matter my true feelings about this.
You write me off as if I don't exist.

I drop my head and turn away,
trusting God for a better day.

Oh boy, I hurt deep down inside.
Is there really anyone in whom I can confide?
Is there a bandage for a bleeding heart?
Hurt showed me just where to ponder and start.
It pointed the way to a moment in time,
a time where everything, all things would be fine.

All the way back to Jesus' death on the cross,
a decision made to save the hurt and the lost.

As I read and study the outcome of this miraculous One,
I look squarely at hurt and say, "You are done."

"Thank you for serving and prepping my life.
You are no longer welcome. I see the light."

My mistakes, shortcomings, and orchestrated doom,
had to take place in order to make room.

Room for Him to be able to work in and through me.
He will not use just any hands or feet.

His way requires many trials and tests,
true confirmation that all has been addressed.

Now I am ready for whatever may arrive.
God's at work. No worries this time.

I think in my mind, He just showed up
because things are better or not as rough.

That's not true. He has always been there,
shaping and molding my life down here.

Oftentimes, God use what's available at the time.
He knows there is victory at the end of the line.
Hurt did its job. I will never be the same.
God removed my fears and my emotions are being tamed.

God, you really do know what's needed and best.
I'm your child now, no longer a hot mess.

Real Help
✝

FIRST	THEN
Romans 3:23	John 16:33
Romans 6:23	Romans 8:36-37
Romans 5:8	1 John 5:4-5
Romans 10:9	2 Corinthians 8-10,16-18
Romans 10:13	Isaiah 64:8
Romans 5:1	
Romans 8:1	

LIFE OR LIFE STRUGGLE?

You're at bat. Life is on the mound.
The pitch is on the way. Are you prepared? Are you sound?

You swing your bat with utter disgust.
You quickly discover it's a strike, a bust.
You wind up again to prepare for the next.
Life lets it go, and a nasty pitch it is—a mess.

You stand there and watch. You're frozen and stiff,
as if you're at the edge of a Mount Rushmore cliff.
You take a step back to reassess your plan.
You readjust your feet and begin to mutter, "I can."

You're ready once more.
Life throws again, third strike you're out.
Another life fanned,
with the breeze of failure and being dealt a bad hand.

As you turn away, just to ponder the result,
how can progress be made when life has you by the throat?
You can't swallow or speak,
process a thought, or even eat.

This life of mine has had its way.
Is there really a promise of a brand new day?
Promises? No. But covenant? Yes.
Promises can be broken, but a covenant will always stand and pass all tests.
Many years ago, your life was negotiated on the body of Christ.
His blood the ink, His Father the insight.
With acceptance of the truth, real life can begin.
The past is erased. The future's your friend.

Your friend because both of you belong to the same person now…
one plan.
one vision.
one mission.
one vow.

Life still will not be easy,
but fortunately, easy is not the goal.
Being a conqueror on earth
requires courage and being bold.

Bold enough to know
who is really running the show.
It's not about what you see,
and all about who and what you know.

Now that things are in order
and divine leadership is aligned,
I have new weapons
and a fully renewed mind.

Life, bring your fight.
Take your best shot,
and watch your mess be carried out
on a Love and Grace cot.

God is my Father.
Mercy is my friend.
Faith is my weapon,
and Jesus fixed sin.

The Holy Spirit is my power,
and hope keeps things exciting.
This life is worth living
although it involves some fighting.

When you have all power
supporting your punch,
realizing you've won
is more than a hunch.

Thank you, Father,
for revealing real life.
Thank you, world,
for the contribution to insight.

Real Help

✝

FIRST	THEN
Romans 3:23	John 16:33
Romans 6:23	Psalm 121:1-2
Romans 5:8	James 1:12
Romans 10:9	Psalm 46:1
Romans 10:13	John 10:10
Romans 5:1	
Romans 8:1	

WAKE UP

Your eyes are open. Your vision is clear.
Your mind is blank, no thoughts appear.
You're physically present, all faculties intact.
Truth is, you are sleep walking, no kidding, all fact.

You decide to quit school to start a career,
doing something that can only be done in fear,
fear of being caught because it's against the law.
Wake up my friend before you are taught
that modern-day crime still results in fines
which may include a lifetime of you doing time.

Ladies, wake up and stop the fuss.
You think you are entitled because you have a nice butt.
Yes, that bubble can stir up much trouble.
Guys peddling lies, just for an appointment to meet with those thighs.

Because of all this, you think you're it.
Fools acting crazy and you are having a fit.
Real ladies know what matters most.
What's really important and worthy of boast.

Having a nice body is really great,
but only as bait that leads to character traits.
She knows her "fine" is really her mind,
a series of right choices matured over time.

She is constantly modeling self-respect and self-control,
knowing that virtuous beauty is the target and goal.
She is aware that life requires understanding and insight,
a necessary combination in order to live it right.

To even think your body is the answer to it all,
will result in disaster and a costly fall.

Yes, it's true. Some recover just fine.
The question is, will you strike luck when it's your time?
Luck it will be because with blind chances, there's no guarantees.

Ladies, wake up and be who you are:
strong, gentle and blessed from afar.
You are God's precious flower, constantly in bloom,
spreading His love in every tune.

Whether it's a song of dread, or a rhythm of delight,
love sings victory, no matter the plight.

Alright, men, it's time to wake up too.
The numbers are adding up, but not in the classroom.
You spend hours in the gym to put on muscle.
You spend more time than that with your boys, planning your next hustle.

The girls are constantly up in your face
because you have a nice car and you're renting your own place.
Because of your smile, confidence, and finesse,
bedding a different woman was never a stretch.

What you didn't know was, you've created a mess,
a life forever altered by a positive HIV test.
Did you really think being "The Man" was free?
That you could work for the devil and not pay a fee?
All those honeys you thought you drew
were part of the mission to help ruin you.
Now you're awake and fully aware
that life is not playing and bad decisions stare,
back at you from consequence row,
a place of no escape, regardless of where you go.

Consequences are also teachers of life.
Learn to listen and obtain insight.
You were created long ago to obtain victory through your mind.
That is where the battle is won or lost every time.

So, see, consequences were never supposed to be your guide.
That's just the devil and all his lies.
Now renew your mind and become acquainted with truth,
by asking God to accept and save you.
He's waiting patiently on you to do just that,
to fulfill His promise to all who ask.

WAKE UP!

Real Help

✝

FIRST		THEN
Romans 3:23		Romans 12:1-2
Romans 6:23		1 Corinthians 6:19-20
Romans 5:8		1 Samuel 16:7
Romans 10:9		Ephesians 2:10
Romans 10:13		John 8:44
Romans 5:1		
Romans 8:1		

DEARLY BELOVED

You were never wanted, at least that's been said.
I know that's a lie, because I wrote what was read.
Your birth was intentional and thoroughly planned out.
The rocky start means nothing. My Son suffered similar bouts.

Your father checked out. Your mother is worn out
from trying to do a job that requires two.
It seems as if your life is doomed.
So, get accustomed to it, you are going nowhere soon.

Do you really think I would leave you like this?
No chance to live and experience true bliss?
I know all about those who are failing you now,
those ones that enjoy turning your smile upside down.

Every plan has a beginning, middle, and end.
Just know that I am controlling your life, my friend.
You see, things are controlled and managed by time.
I own it all, and yes, time is mine.

It has to obey and do what I say.
So, rest in peace and tell concern to "Cease."
You think I am unaware of your efforts down there,
trying for success and avoiding all the mess.

Just keep on working and disregard what you see.
When you do that, then you will see me,
arranging and orchestrating something larger than you,
a window of love that all can see through.

I've had you by the hand the entire time.

God's Answer to Life Struggles

I have always been there to ensure you're fine.
The rough moments were allowed in order to build a foundation,
to enable you to support, my future contemplation.

Your parents' assignment was complete the day you arrived.
I took it from there. I've kept you alive.
If you take a minute and stop and think,
how did you move those mountains, being so weak?

How did that bullet bypass your brain?
When it was shot intentionally at point blank range?
Do you think luck just suddenly showed up?
Or maybe your reflexes resulted in a very quick duck?

I was there when it all went down.
I made gravity multiply and ordered the bullet to ground.
My love for you requires that I protect your life.
We are in this together, but it's still My fight.

Don't ever worry about what the future holds.
Good, bad, and ugly are mixed in the same bowl.
That's irrelevant because I control the goal.

Since love is my reason and you're a part of my plan,
nothing else matters, so, relax and stand.
While you stand and contemplate, allow your mind to be soothed.
Oh, by the way, I'm God and I'm referring to you.

Real Help

✝

FIRST	THEN
Romans 3:23	Deuteronomy 31:6
Romans 6:23	1 John 5:4
Romans 5:8	Isaiah 26:3
Romans 10:9	Philippians 4:13
Romans 10:13	Isaiah 40:28-31
Romans 5:1	Colossians 3:23
Romans 8:1	

HAPPILY MISLED

The sun is shining. The birds are singing.
The bees are roaming from flower to flower, no stinging.
My feet hit the floor. I am ready to go.
It's another day available for me to go make some dough.

I am really good at what I do.
I can steal the sole from a shoe without bothering the glue.
It is hard to believe I've been given these skills.
I can take advantage of anyone, no joke, for real.

It's a wholesome treat to accomplish these feats.
My conscious is clear and I have no fear.

Just the other day I was at a penthouse.
I was laughing and drinking with someone else's spouse.
We began to talk. She shared some faults.
My plan was at work. She's about to be taught.

When the day was over, I had my fun.
Another one conquered, another one done.
It's really a shame how good I am,
the way I rocked her in spite of her man.

Life is good on every side.
It's hard to imagine an end to this ride.
While living it up and keeping it real,
I met some important people during a business deal.
We talked about the present and how to make the future grand.
I was happy to discover my skills still in demand.
Bold, confident, no conscious, and quick hands.

We discussed some details, then I was on my way.
I was equipped with it all, to land a big payday.
I followed the instructions to the letter, at least I thought.
When I made the exchange, we all got caught.

The penthouse, the lady, the fun I had,
was all a set up to accomplish this bad.
The meeting, my skills, and being a confident fool,
was more than enough to end my rule.

I was having a ball. Everything was fine.
Enjoying the present, the future was mine.
It's really strange how wisdom can come,
when the party is over and there's no more fun.

Being misled and happy too,
is like walking barefoot on broken glass while owning many pair shoes.

I remember when I
was just a little kid.
I was reading a book,
and this is what it said,

"Be careful of the things you say and do,
because it will definitely come back to you."
Bad or good, mean or nice,
your choices set the course for what happens in your life.

If you ever need or want help with what to choose,
just contact me and I will gladly direct you.
Who am I? I am glad you asked.
I'm God, your creator. I know what's best!

Real Help
✝

FIRST	THEN
Romans 3:23	Philippians 2:3, Genesis 1:1
Romans 6:23	Galatians 6:7-8
Romans 5:8	Ephesians 4:28
Romans 10:9	Leviticus 19:11
Romans 10:13	Proverbs 10:2
Romans 5:1	Proverbs 16:18
Romans 8:1	James 1:5

WORRY

It has been quite a while since I've had some peace.
My finances and health seem to always concern me.
I cannot remember the last time I got a full night's rest.
I wake suddenly throughout the night, alarmed and distressed.

I tell myself, it's only concern.
When things aren't right, it's just my turn.
My turn to take, the medicine of life,
a life that requires me to scuffle and fight.

I know it has to be this way.
I watched my parents have to pay.
They paid with their health, resulting in frustration and very little wealth.
I watched them give up and place their hope on a shelf.

It seemed only right to emulate their plight,
giving in to what seemed to be their only mental glean.
Concern is fine. It's a natural part of life.
However, it should never cause trouble or result in sleepless nights.

The true culprit is worry and it's not your friend.
It was sent from your enemy, to do you in.
Satan is the one behind this smoking gun!

He knows what he is doing,
quite aware of every ingredient, in the concoction he's brewing.
He is on a mission to change your focus and adjust your decisions.
He knows that worry puts pressure on the mind.
It eats away slowly, causing damage over time.
Stress, hypertension, and ulcers too,
only a few reminders that worry has you.

This list is small but far from complete.
What about the time you had swelling in your feet?
Worrying all night long, put pressure on your heart.
Your vessels failed, causing a leak to start.

Worry is bad news, just examine the clues.
You thought it was concern designed to teach and help you learn.
Now that you know, this has to stop.
Is there a key that can fit this lock?

The key of truth is all that's required.
Faith is the answer for the methods of a liar.
For all the times you worried all night,
faith was waiting for an invitation to the fight.

Faith is the reason that worry has no power.
God says faith in Him is a strong tower.
God has addressed every situation and crisis.
Then He briefed faith with all the answers to satan's vices.

Satan is well aware of what faith can do.
Why do you think he works so hard at misleading you?
Worry is just one of the weapons he uses,
but faith is the nemesis of whatever he chooses.

Have faith in God's evaluation,
of every situation.
By doing this,
you disarm the risk,
of being a victim on satan's long list.

Now that you know what's lie and truth,
what you do from here is all up to you.

Real Help

✝

FIRST	THEN
Romans 3:23	Philippians 4:6-7
Romans 6:23	Isaiah 41:10
Romans 5:8	1 Peter 5:7
Romans 10:9	John 8:44
Romans 10:13	Hebrews 11:1,6
Romans 5:1	
Romans 8:1	

DEATH ROW

When you think of being sentenced and awaiting execution,
those behind bars generate the mental intrusion.
The death row mentality is more relative than you think.
Give life some thought, look closely, and don't blink.

All the way back during your time of conception,
chromosomes were given—they were all infected, no exceptions.
Being genetically flawed, creates a real problem,
because life was meant to be enjoyed, not to just be a bother.

Being a recipient of a sinful bloodline
means death is your lot, and hell your final stop.
The Bible records, Adam committed high treason.
Dealing every human being a real good reason
to question morality and promote self-pleasing.

The truth of the matter is, we were all born on death row,
an object of betrayal from a deadly foe.
The day our lives started, they began to end.
The clock started the countdown and our lives started to descend.

A situation much different than the original plan,
see, man was created to live forever in this great land.
One selfish decision affected us all.
Now hard times, death, and the grave are the consequence of that fall.

Have you ever wondered why things get better just to get worse?
How about the fact that the last never seem to end up being first?
The rich seem to always just take even more.
The poor are always, just that, they're poor.

It's an infinite cycle of ups and downs.
If you stay on this course, while your feet are on the ground,
death is your reward and to hell you are bound.

Is it right for this to be my plight?
I had nothing at all to do with my birthright.

Being born this way doesn't mean you have to stay.
Jesus' death on the cross erased Adam's broken way.
He did it all so you wouldn't have to pay.

The price required to set you free,
required pure blood not infected by you and me.

Accept Jesus Christ as Savior and Lord.
He will give you His blood in exchange for yours.
A new bloodline results in a brand new person.
You will now use your mouth for praise instead of cursing.

The best news of all is your salvation from this world and its unrelenting destruction.
Your new life will come equipped with brand new instructions.

The end will come, but for you that'll be fun.
You will no longer have to gamble with life's loaded gun.

Just to think about those who remain on death row,
and realize there is a way off by just saying "NO."
My heart is saddened and I get upset,
because I know that my pardon is also the answer to their debt.
Jesus shed enough blood to transfuse us all.
You can do something about it, before the last call.
Now you know your condition and the resolution too.
Call on Jesus and let Him save you!

Real Help

✟

FIRST	THEN
Romans 3:23	Hebrews 9:27
Romans 6:23	Genesis 3:19
Romans 5:8	Romans 5:12-21
Romans 10:9	John 3:16
Romans 10:13	
Romans 5:1	
Romans 8:1	

BLESSED

Blessed are those who are awake in Christ.
He gave you many gifts to win life's fight.
He blessed your mind with renewed thoughts.
Your soul is blessed because He went to the cross.

Your spirit is blessed with the ambiance of His presence,
the gift of His glory, the awareness of His essence.
Your body is blessed to endure life's journey.
Be a good steward and take care of God's yearning.

Your conscious is blessed with the word of God,
sprinkled with His blood, doing good is no longer hard.
Though a challenge, it's already done.
Remember what Jesus did; the battle is already won.

Your heart is blessed because it's been newly changed.
It still pumps blood, but it's not the same.
The blood from this heart is mixed with love,
prepared in heaven, sent from above.

With the spoon of the Holy Spirit stirring in mercy and grace,
faith begins to take its rightful place.
Blessed are those walking in this boldness.
The result is a loving warmness, not the world's everyday coldness.

It's true that blessings rest on the unjust as well.
With hell being a real place, you can settle and fail.
A Christian is blessed regardless of the circumstance,
because God is the leader on this eternal dance.

Whether it's a slow waltz

or a frantic hustle,
God can handle it.
He's the strength, the muscle.

Enjoy being blessed, a gift of heavenly favor.
Some things are reserved for heaven's future neighbors.
All who are blessed will live together in the end,
when Jesus comes back to receive all of His kin.

Thank God for being blessed.
Thank God. Amen.
I REST!!!

Real Help

✟

FIRST	THEN
Romans 3:23	Ephesians 1:3-5
Romans 6:23	Psalm 32:1-2
Romans 5:8	Psalm 146:5
Romans 10:9	Psalm 84:11-13
Romans 10:13	2 Corinthians 9:8-10
Romans 5:1	1 Peter 4:10
Romans 8:1	

LIFE

A slow breath in through your nose
now, relax and let it flow.
What a precious feeling of excitement of life on the go.

As oxygen slowly moves through the body taking notes,
it reminds all the organs of its ability to cope,
with whatever situation that may happen, no joke!

Close your eyes and reminisce.
Lend some thought to your very first kiss.
Somewhat sloppy but patiently waited for,
a feeling of warmth, a desiring to soar.

As life goes on, situations change.
Maturity knocks on the door as adolescence is shackled and carried away in chains.
Mother nature starts to visit on a regular basis,
causing changes in your life, leaving her results in strange places.

The body begins to change, the mind starts to wake up.
You desire interaction, you are through with going Dutch.
The things you once thought were a waste of time,
begin to make sense, all of a sudden, they're fine.

With life's serving change from every direction, trying to do right is only a deflection.
You try to go left, you end up right. You try to stay loose, you end up tight.
Why so complex this life we endure?
Just to turn on every side and find a closed door.
What a paradox, at least it seems.
You have to dig deeper if you want to glean.
The original blueprint wasn't written this way.
God had other plans, a panacea, no dismay.

Kenneth E. Piper

Man decided to exercise his will,
a decision that served everyone a raw deal.
With Adam's decision, all had to pay.
With Jesus' decision, it's never too late.

Life is not about the struggles in a day,
the times you gave up and said, "There's no way."
It's all about letting Jesus control your life.
He's the answer to it all, from cancer to strife.

Life doesn't have to rest in an abyss of hard times.
Jesus is a refuge against all penalties and fines.

Life has a glow for all those who know
that Heaven is aware of what's happening down here.

When life starts with God, it will never end.
Eternally in His care, you are safely tucked within.
So, life have your way and do your best.
Jesus is the master and has the answers to all your tests.

You're Blessed!

Real Help

✝

FIRST	THEN
Romans 3:23	John 16:33
Romans 6:23	1 John 5:4-5
Romans 5:8	John 14:6
Romans 10:9	
Romans 10:13	
Romans 5:1	
Romans 8:1	

TEARS

The funeral is over.
Now the real battle begins.
They are no longer around
to help you make amends.

For many, many days
you relied on their wisdom.
I hope you kept notes
because now you are going to need them.

Although they are saved,
the tears continue for days and days.
As the waters flow across the windows of your soul,
weeping is strength. Jesus did it. It's bold.

The verdict is "Guilty." The sentence is "Life."
The attorney was paid to give away your rights.
Knowing your innocence and your alibi is true,
remember your brother Joseph, he went through this too.

Even though tears are falling and life's a blur,
deep in your mind you say, "How could this occur?"
With a struggle in your mind, you leave your life behind.
You've forgotten God has a plan, all in due time.

You come home early from a hard day's work.
Your boss has been unbelievable, an outright jerk.
As you approach your door, you hear familiar sounds,
moaning and groaning, someone's getting down.

The closer you get, your heart starts to race.

You say to yourself, "I'm the only one authorized to love in this place."
As you approach the scene, your heart starts to scream.
Tears began to roll. This situation is cold.

You are out making a living. Your spouse is out giving,
serving someone else your marriage plate, thinking you will be home a little late.

Your tears distort the vision of a beautiful wedding day.
Your heart is broken, you are filled with dismay.
The transformation has started. Your mind shifts gears.
Hurt is in order, in the midst of your tears.

The Holy Spirit takes over and it's good He did
because only He can walk away and let these two live.
This is painful. You wish you could breathe.
You can't seem to make it. You fall to your knees.

You pray your prayer and see what follows.
The Lord answers and gathers your tears in a bottle.
"Don't worry, my child, about this terrible mess.
All things work together in the end for the best.

Always remember that your tears of pain and sorrow
serve as a down payment on a brand new tomorrow, tomorrow, tomorrow…"

Real Help
✟

FIRST	THEN
Romans 3:23	Psalm 56:8
Romans 6:23	Psalm 55:22
Romans 5:8	1 Peter 5:7
Romans 10:9	Romans 12:19
Romans 10:13	Luke 6:27-28
Romans 5:1	1 Thessalonians 5:16-18
Romans 8:1	

SURPRISE

That special day is here. A long wait is finally at rest.
Everyone is present, all family and guests.
Secluded behind the scenes, you ponder and glean,
Will it all live up to what it really means?

Is this a big day to celebrate God's grace,
Or just a day hidden in satan's place?

Is there understanding in what we are demanding?
Do we truly know what rests beneath the flow?
Do we have what it takes to mend life's breaks?
Do we have Christ's heart that endures beyond the start?

Flippantly, the questions are answered with a resounding "YES,"
not considering that soon, there will be test.
A necessary meeting to reveal the truth,
Are we genuine or just a ruse?

Surprises are victorious when you are not prepared.
In the heat of the moment, you didn't know they would go there.
Expressions change, words fly,
the heart is revealed, and hopes die.

The situation starts to paint a picture of its own,
a portrait of reality that's been present all along.
Since the heart is involved, acceptance is tough.
Could it be true that I've been bamboozled, I've been bluffed?
This can't be true. This can't be real.
There was a lot of time and effort invested in this deal.

What happened to love? How can it die,

when Jesus lives and can never lie?
Love is all that God says it is.
That includes all the promises to those who are His.

People choose to be far less than what God intended.
God knew that, so He sent Jesus to mend it.

Real Help

✝

FIRST	THEN
Romans 3:23	Proverbs 3:5-6
Romans 6:23	1 Chronicles 28:9
Romans 5:8	Romans 8:28
Romans 10:9	
Romans 10:13	
Romans 5:1	
Romans 8:1	

FRIENDSHIP

When life is good and the sun is shining,
it's quite alright to enjoy good timing.
When you see my mistakes and your smile is fake,
I thought you were my friend. Be real for God's sake!

I am all tied up in the midst of my mess.
Your pat on my back just signals you could care less.
What I really need is a swift kick in the seat.
Start being my friend. That would be neat!

Don't let me off the hook
until my life resembles the "Good Book."
Be my friend, exactly what I need,
not just a body that smiles, nods, and agrees.

Being a true friend means finding fault with sin,
especially since we're spiritual kin.
True friendship is precious and hard to find,
so don't ever stop holding me accountable for the wrongs that are mine.

Please do your part in being my friend.
I am mature enough to handle what happens in the end.

When you have played your part
in helping complete what God intended from the start,
God gets the glory,
and we both get a changed heart.
The intent of all of this is not to offend.
It is all about the necessity of being a friend.

Thank you. Thank you. Thank you. My friend.

Real Help
✠

FIRST	THEN
Romans 3:23	Proverbs 17:17
Romans 6:23	Proverbs 18:24
Romans 5:8	Proverbs 27:17
Romans 10:9	1 Corinthians 15:33
Romans 10:13	Proverbs 27:6
Romans 5:1	Psalm 141:5
Romans 8:1	

BELIEVE

Life will always present situations of concern.
What you believe determines which direction you will turn.
What is fueling that train of thought?
Experience, emotion, circumstance, or God's Law?

It's very easy to evaluate and figure that out.
God gives you peace. All others, just doubt.
What troubles you deep down inside?
That situation, that decision, that thing you've chosen to hide?

What does God say about your secret torments?
Those tasty morsels of hidden lament?
Believe in God's ability to love and suffice,
regardless of the situation, circumstance, or price.

Belief is a challenge when you don't let God manage.
God's promises are true. They are mini love notes written to and for you.
Don't allow the world to shake or shape your core.
Just pray and believe and allow heaven to keep score.

God's word is truth, an immovable rock.
Regardless of the outcome, you will end up on top.
The object of your faith determines your destination.
By not choosing Jesus, you choose devastation.

But believing in Him changes everything to "new."
He purchased your life because He believes in you.
Believe in God. It's about Him and you.
Everything else is dead, done, and through.

When you've done all you can, just stand and believe in the Son of man.

The end result has been written.
God's plan will stand!

Real Help

✚

FIRST	THEN
Romans 3:23	Romans 10:11,17
Romans 6:23	Mark 11:24
Romans 5:8	Proverbs 23:7
Romans 10:9	2 Corinthians 5:17
Romans 10:13	Psalm 144:1-2
Romans 5:1	
Romans 8:1	

ANGER

As I look in the mirror and stare into my eyes,
I'm ashamed to admit the inferno inside.
When I think of the problems and challenges I face,
My blood vessels constrict, leaving very little space…for blood to flow.
I'm about to blow.

With a hot head and troubled mind,
I am dangerously close to murder this time.
Why can't I seem to get a grip?
Instead I end up with red eyes and a busted lip.

Being wounded is one thing, but being dead is another.
I can't keep hiding behind my manhood as a cover.
It's getting harder to keep this genie in the bottle.
People seem to know that I have anger problems.

As I walk around with a smile on my face,
Way down deep is where the real story takes place.
The smile is really a "NO TRESPASS" sign.
If you disregard the message, there is always a fine.

The price may vary from a bruised ego or your life.
You choose to enter and give fate a try.
Though I smile in silence, your antics increase,
As if you have no problems with me springing a leak.

What you don't know about is the conversation I am having with my conscious.
There is a battle going on, and believe me, it's monstrous!
A battle to keep me from grabbing you by the throat
And increasing the pressure while I watch you choke.

Being that you are the one that caused this mess,
Remember my smile when I was trying to avoid this unrest.
The world would understand why all this happened,
But being a Christian means I was clearly caught napping.

See, the Bible teaches to be led by the Spirit
And never allow your conscious or the world to make your decisions.
A smile on our faces should symbolize love,
A love that is always controlled from above.

We do not smile because we enjoy ridicule or discomfort.
We just remember who promised to control dysfunction.
It really does not matter how bad things get.
God has evaluated and promised peace in the midst.

A promise from God has already been fulfilled,
So claim it for yourself and transform what's real.
See, God sent promises to proclaim over your life.
He knew that anger would be a big cause of our strife.

God knows that when you rip off the mask of anger
with love, it reveals the true culprit,
the actual hand in the glove.

Pride is the real reason that nothing is fine.
Anger is the scapegoat that gets the attention every time.
Pride says, "I want it now. I want it my way."
Anger shows up when there is a delay.

Anger is the fuel that keeps the motor of pride running.
Don't allow these two the satisfaction of being cunning.
Love is the answer to the problems of anger.
God provides the love to disarm that stranger.

So, remember that you were created for love and peace.
You were created in His image. He is always at ease.

Operate in this truth and never give in to doubt.
Take a deep breath. It is already worked out.

Real Help

✝

FIRST	THEN
Romans 3:23	Psalm 37:8
Romans 6:23	Proverbs 29:11,22
Romans 5:8	Proverbs 14:17,29
Romans 10:9	Romans 12:21
Romans 10:13	Proverbs 11:2
Romans 5:1	Proverbs 16:5
Romans 8:1	

Long Distance

Today's technology is impressive, to say the least.
We have computers, robots, and phones that can teach.
We are able to stream information from satellites in the sky,
regardless of the cost or who had to die.

It's amazing what people will do or pay just to be able to talk all day.
Discussions take place from the town hall to the shopping mall.

Communication is power and it certainly is not cheap.
When was the last time your phone call was free?
This world has found a way to place a price tag on your right to speak.
It's a cash cow that is binding for you and for me.

Why pay so much for this useless chatter?
The most important calls are free, so let's discuss the matter.
Have you ever received the bills for the phone calls you've made to heaven?
The time your child was missing and God told you to check his room at seven?

Remember that strange call
a few days after you lost your job?
God informed you of a much better situation
Because working there you were being robbed.

Remember the night God revealed the devil's lie,
right before you made an attempt at suicide?
Let's not forget about all the calls throughout the day,
just for Him to say, "I love you," and remind you of His grace.
It doesn't matter where you are
or your present condition.
God charges nothing,
because saving a life is not about a job but all about His mission!

A mission that distance can't even impact,
because with God, distance evaporates like water off a duck's back.

God says that everyone loves the sound of free,
but many will perish because they will not call me.
What I offer is out of this world.
Allow me to explain and watch it unfurl.

When you call me, the line is never busy.
I answer it personally, no machines to cause a tizzy.
It really does not matter about your native tongue.
I speak and understand every language under the sun.

I never have a need to place you on hold.
I am self-sufficient with no needs to control.
You can call me, anytime, day or night.
I never sleep, get tired, or become uptight.

Regardless of the concern, I have the solution.
I know all there is to know. I even know the future.
Every situation has already been resolved.
I fixed it all, when I went to the cross.

So, now you have heard what I have to say.
I am always available to all who pray.
I want to hear from you, so do not make me wait.
The moment you speak my name, I am there to address the case.

Do not worry about what you see.
Remember, it's all about faith in what you believe.
As great as earthly technology can be,
remember it can never accomplish what I offer for free.

Get to know me, the only universal key.
I am the creator and architect of everything you see.

Real Help

✝

FIRST	THEN
Romans 3:23	Jeremiah 10:12-13
Romans 6:23	2 Peter 1:3
Romans 5:8	1 Corinthians 1:9
Romans 10:9	Genesis 1:1
Romans 10:13	Isaiah 45:12
Romans 5:1	
Romans 8:1	

FORGIVENESS

It has been 15 years since I've spoken to my sister.
I know that sounds bad, but personally I'm glad.

I still cannot believe she did me that way.
How can your own blood set you up to pay?
Serves her right that life has been tough.
If I had my way, I would include some rough.

I heard my dad is very sick right now.
How is that news supposed to make me frown?
The way I see it, he is getting what he gave.
He left when I was a baby, so proceed on to the grave.

He never even checked to see if I was alive.
I will not waste my time on that empathy jive.
I will never forget what he did, or should I say didn't do for me.
He deserves to suffer, so leave me be!

Church is a joke.
I grew up in there with all those religious folks.
The entire time I was serving among the Godly,
one of the teachers was teaching me the operation of my body.

That person spoke so eloquently while among the masses,
but behind the scenes, I was given private classes.
Now my mind is all messed up.
Trying to be in any relationship is close to impossible and awfully tough.
I have a major problem with sincerity and disgust with trust.

The day I got married, I meant what I said.
My spouse would be the only one to ever share my bed.
With hopes of a future filled with great expectations,

I cannot believe my spouse surrendered so easily to temptation.

Now I am broken.
I am extremely upset.
We were both Christians.
How could this happen to the ones who are in God's nest?

The above situations don't even scratch the surface of the pain,
misery, and dysfunction going on while living on earth—a modern day circus.
No matter the foe,
if you will pay the price, you can see the show.

If you like what you see, joining in is free.
But be forewarned, nothing is ever really free.
You pay with your life at the expense of what you see.

Truth is extremely valuable,
regardless of the price.
It is the very thing that God uses
to bless and extend life.

The truth of the matter is
we live every day in a sin sick world.
That's the real reason bad situations happen
to men, women, boys, and girls.

Regardless of your condition or circumstance,
there is a way to start over and activate a new plan.
Get to know Jesus.
He gives you much more than eternal life.
He gives you His love to make everything alright.

You are right. There is no way you can do it on your own.
That was never His plan when He ascended to the throne.

His love includes the incredible ability to forgive.

A spiritual gift that helps you live.
It helps you live a victorious life,
regardless of whether things are wrong or right.

See, forgiving someone for the wrong they have done,
is not agreeing with the ordeal or supposed to be fun.
It is really a way of freeing yourself.
Unforgiveness affects everything including your health.

We need God's help in every aspect of our life.
Unforgiveness is the culprit that removes Him from the fight.
He will not forgive us if we will not forgive others.
Why allow someone else to interfere with your access to being spiritually covered?

Forgiveness is God's way of making things right.
It opens a door that requires spiritual sight.
Being someone in need of forgiveness too,
God knows this is the best way that He can take care of you.

We can never receive what we will not give.
God gave first, allowing you to live.
While hanging on the cross, Jesus prayed a forgiveness prayer,
while all of His persecutors made fun, mocked, and stared.

He did it that way as an example for us all.
He knew that forgiveness is the only answer for those who stumble and fall.
Unforgiveness always answers with negatives and the problem.
Forgiveness focuses on who can solve what bothers.

Unforgiveness leads to resentment which causes a hardened heart.
Forgiveness breaks this chain and provides a fresh start.
Forgiveness is always God's answer to a dilemma.
It is the only way He gets the chance to make all involved, winners.

God will help you forgive all that has been done.
I am sure that nothing compares to what was done to His Son!

Real Help

✝

FIRST	THEN
Romans 3:23	Mark 11:25
Romans 6:23	Matthew 6:14-15
Romans 5:8	Colossians 3:12-13
Romans 10:9	Romans 12:19-21
Romans 10:13	Ephesians 4:31-32
Romans 5:1	Mark 14:65
Romans 8:1	Matthew 27:32-56

LOVE = CHRIST

Love has been accused
of the reason for people being abused.
The meaning of love has been sorely mistreated.
How can love be the reason for people being defeated?

Love has been bruised and poorly represented.
Love and hate should never occupy the same sentence.
Saying "I love you" has become an empty anthem or meaningless chant.
God is saddened because love is everything, but surely not that.

To experience love's true meaning, you have to forget what you know.
See, love is a person and not emotions and thoughts that flow to and fro.
It is amazing how the word love has been misused.
It's almost as if it were a trick or a ruse.

The love of money has caused a man to leave his wife.
The love for status and prestige has caused all sorts of unrest and strife.
The word love has been used for the same sex to enter a lie.
Calling themselves married, but God will address that misfire as He desires.

Love has been accused of every wrong under the sun.
Love is not the problem. Foolish people are the ones.
True love resides in one person alone.
Jesus is love, and without Him, it's gone.

I am sure that many will claim to be an expert on this subject,
but let's get the truth from God and let's not get it from the public.
See, love started long ago when Jesus died on the cross.
You do know that nails did not keep Him there, it was His love for the lost.

The true standard of love is Jesus himself.

Study His life and experience love for yourself.
Real love is about service and help,
a process of allowing God to love through you for the benefit of someone else.

True love always looks and feels the same.
Jesus is the reason and lovingkindness is His claim.
Every situation can be resolved with Christian love.
Knowing all things, enable Jesus to perfectly rise above,
see the real picture, and give the whole thing a hug.

Once He analyzes everything right,
Then He provides guidance and spiritual insight.
There is a process that takes place when you accept Jesus Christ into your life.
His Spirit lives in you and now love is resident on site.

Regardless of the situation, love can be your guide.
He is right there eternally, living inside.
Anger, disgust, fear, and the like,
they all have to surrender because His love holds all might.

Love is all about showing this world who Jesus is.
Since He and love are one in the same,
let's get His perspective and dispel all shame.

First of all, love has little to do with emotions and how one feels.
It is all about obedience and commitment of the will.
The will to emulate Christ,
regardless to who is wrong or right.

True love makes a decision before an offense takes place.
It says" yes" to God's way, regardless of the price that has to be paid.
Love is patient. Love is kind.
But not quite like the world defines.

Being patient and kind according to Christ
doesn't result in change because someone threatens your life.

In that very moment, His power shows up most.
See, love like this requires the Holy Ghost.

A supernatural Spirit of unconditional love,
this kind of love only comes from above.
Love like this can endure all things.
It provides God's viewpoint, equipped with His team.

You begin to realize that love requires a journey with God as your guide.
Regardless of the difficulty or distance of this ride,
He will remain faithful, right by your side.

Love is God's method of caring for all,
not just those who have accepted His call.
Jesus died for all to have the chance,
to live, love, and walk like He can.

There is nothing this world can conjure up
that this type of love cannot interrupt.
Christ's love is superior because it's an extension of Him.
Nothing else can begin to contend.

Since this world is filled with hatred and chaos,
without real love you're as good as lost.
Christ is waiting to be love in our life.
He knows what is needed to make all wrongs, right.
Do you really want to experience real love and all of its hype?
Give up the world system and give your life to Christ.
Jesus is waiting. He's already said "Yes."
He knows how to love and care for you best.

Do not leave this world without experiencing true love.
It's a shame to live a lifetime and never experience His hug.

Real Help

✝

FIRST	THEN
Romans 3:23	1 John 4:16
Romans 6:23	1 John 4:8
Romans 5:8	1 Corinthians 13
Romans 10:9	
Romans 10:13	
Romans 5:1	
Romans 8:1	

LOVE ALL OVER ME

The brilliance of my smile,
the glare within my eyes,
joy is on display,
even when I cry.

The extra beat of my heart, a brand new start,
I never imagined that this could happen for me.
After all, I was given away when I was around three.

It all turned out to be a beginning filled with promise.
Regardless of how it started, I have always been on God's compass.

A blood guarantee from true royalty.
A decision that was made before I was even me.

I look up into the infinite skies
to embrace a glare, face to face with God's eyes.
He stretched out His arms, bowed His head and surrendered His life,
to let me see that His love is spread all over me.

Struggles begin to mount.
Hard times multiply beyond count.
Overwhelmed by life's vicious cycle, love seems nonexistent,
because time and trouble has got me all twisted.

A single word from Him,
saying life, time, and trouble, don't worry about them.
They work for me,
constantly assisting in you being free.

My love for you

always trumps that crew.
Twisted no more, I began to focus my mind,
clearly on Him, no distractions this time.

Being reminded that life has many phases, factions, and pitfalls,
with His love on me, I can defeat them all.
No weapon shall prosper; a message to steady my soul.
I have already won for you. Make me your goal.
I will do just that now that I know.

Although life can change and times get tough,
knowing you are loved can silence that fuss.
This type of love is easy to see.
Just watch and witness His love all over me.
I am starting to understand the power of that man,
the depth of His love and purpose of His plan.
Love is the answer to all questions in life.
Give in to it now. Don't struggle. Don't fight.

His love is victory over pain and defeat.
That applies to you too. I'm just talking about me.
If you have not figured out this type of love yet,
his name is Jesus. Now you've met!

Kenneth E. Piper

Real Help
✟

FIRST	THEN
Romans 3:23	John 3:16
Romans 6:23	Isaiah 54:17
Romans 5:8	2 Chronicles 20:15
Romans 10:9	Romans 2:11
Romans 10:13	
Romans 5:1	
Romans 8:1	

STRUGGLE

I'm saved! I'm saved! Thank God almighty, I'm saved!
My life is secure. My way has been paved.

Satan gets the news. He's really upset;
not happy that his plans will never be met.
Now, demons have been assigned to your life for all time.
It's about to get rough, but remember, you're fine.

The battle begins with those who are close;
the very special ones who are around you most.
You try to walk in your newness of life,
no longer being controlled by the things of night.
Night and dark versus day and light.

One represents bad. The other represents good.
God's do's, and the devil's should's.
When you are in the light, everything is clear.
You can see your way, how to operate down here.

When there is something to do and you can't see the way,
shine light on the subject by beginning to pray.
Answers will come straight from the father Himself.
He knows what to do when His children need help.

The devil will always meddle in your lives,
with options, suggestions, and outright lies.
He hopes you will disregard your Christian ties.
Getting you to do the wrong thing is his primary goal,
so he can run back and report the whole,
situation to God as if to sway
His decision to remain your savior always.

Kenneth E. Piper

The devil knows his day of reckoning is near.
That's why he kicked things into high gear.
He wants to destroy everyone he can
by causing struggle and strife between women and man.

His outcome and destiny can never be changed,
using money, sex, and lies, he offers the same.
Your decision to accept seems exciting and fun.
What you do not know, is it's a loaded gun.

You're playing Russian roulette with your life.
The devil calls it fun.
When you make the wrong move,
it's over. You're done!

He knows that time with him means dying with him.
No chance at the life for which Jesus' Blood paid the price.
A paradise that is paid in full
by the only person capable of supernatural pull.

When life and the devil create struggles along the way,
knowing the truth will always set the record straight.

Challenges are certain but struggles are selected.
What you don't know will leave you unprotected,
subject to the devil and all his unprotection.

What God allowed was intended to help you grow,
season your mind, and put you in the know.
Instead, you fight the very thing you need,
a face-to-face conference between you and your deeds.

Since God knew it would turn out like this,
He sent His angels to adjust and assist.
The struggle is over. Love takes its place.
God's in control. I rest my case.

Real Help
✝

FIRST	THEN
Romans 3:23	1 John 3:8
Romans 6:23	John 10:10
Romans 5:8	John 8:44
Romans 10:9	1 Peter 5:7
Romans 10:13	Romans 8:17-18
Romans 5:1	Psalm 27:1
Romans 8:1	

YOU SAID IT FIRST

It's useless for me to keep trying to succeed.
It seems as though I will never have what I need to achieve.
My parents were right to give up in this fight.
Who am I to think I can make wrong, right?

The more I try, it just tightens the noose
around my neck. It's just no use.
I ambitiously attend school and make good grades.
I find that life is more about colors and shades.

In the womb, I did not have a say.
I am innocent. I was born this way.
Why should I be the one who has to pay?

I look at the news and come to the realization
that being of color is a true complication.
The solution chosen to sort it all out
can result in my death, or an infinite route,
of being harassed and treated with no class.
My life is in trouble. I am going nowhere fast.

When I was young, just having fun,
I dreamed that life, would serve and suffice.
It wasn't long before reality landed.
My dreams shattered. I felt abandoned.

I sit quietly in a secluded place.
I'm trying to avoid that face-to-face
encounter with my conscious, a vicious replay,
of my life in reverse, reminding me constantly that I'm living a curse.

A curse that I was taught to speak.
Keep saying what you see and you're stuck with me.
There is a way to save the day.
Only one way, by correcting what you say.

The truth of the matter has already been revealed.
Speak what God says and reverse the deal.
He made some promises that can never be broken.
They are in His word just waiting to be spoken.

He says that you can have what you say.
Instead you choose to reverse it by saying it the opposite way.
You say what you have, so you have what you say.
It should be obvious why no change takes place.

The fact that you've been trained in a lie all your life,
does not exempt you from getting it right.
Those who love you taught only what they knew,
never intending or trying to mislead you.

Now that you've been made aware of God and His plan,
it's your responsibility to take a new stand.
Study God's word and learn His ways.
Acquire wisdom and add joy to your days.

No matter the circumstances or current conditions,
God has always had plans and He always had a mission.
Because He knows everything that concerns your life,
He uses wrong as fuel in your fight.
So, forget the past and bear hug the future.
God is waiting as your guide and tutor.
He wants to impact this world with His love and plans.
Hurry up now. You're His feet and His hands.

Real Help

✝

FIRST	THEN
Romans 3:23	Proverbs 18:21
Romans 6:23	Matthew 12:37
Romans 5:8	Mark 11:23
Romans 10:9	Proverbs 6:2
Romans 10:13	Proverbs 13:3
Romans 5:1	
Romans 8:1	

MY BODY

My vision is clear. I have a plan.
I placed my thoughts in the heart of man.
Ordinary man can never be expected
to accomplish this mission. It is much too eclectic.

The ones that I use are a part of me.
They do the work while I direct and teach.
It seems complex to direct from afar,
but I am God and truly in charge.

When I left the earth, I really did not leave.
I sent my Spirit to save and cleave.
My Spirit saves the lost and adheres to their hearts.
It prepares them for work that I was sent to start.

As people accept me as Lord of their lives,
my body is formed on earth in clear sight.
My body is equipped with everything needed
to transform this world and show satan defeated.

To make things clear,
my body is the church,
not an edifice or building,
but those few on a search.

People who seek after me and my will,
those are the ones who display my seal.
My stamp is love. My seal is my Spirit.
For those who know me can never conceal it.

As a part of my body, they listen and watch.
As God reveals, they react and launch.

This body was created for the purpose of change.
How can God be here and things remain the same?

That could never be because of what He sees.
He has never been one to accept wrong deeds.
When you were sick and had no wellness plan,
someone in His body stepped up and said, "I can."

You never found out how the bill got paid in full.
The truth is, God assigned your case to be pulled.
Remember the times your children gave you fits.
They didn't seem to listen, not even a little bit.
You knew in your heart they were going the wrong way.
You threw up your hands with nothing else to say.
God saw your gesture and pointed them out.
The body started moving and working it out.

On their path to destruction,
they encountered a sign,
that said, "We know who you are,
turn back this time."
A little bit spooked, they heeded the warning.
Sometimes even fools participate in learning.

Being distracted by disgust, you lost your faith.
God saw the problem and stepped in your place.
The sign they saw was an extension of me.
He was dressed in linen with a limp in his knee.
My body's mission is the same as mine,
to save the lost and love the unkind.
My Spirit is always available to you.
Once you accept, I will use you too.

There is no limit to what I can do.
Become a part of me and allow greatness to ensue.
My body starts with me. It can also include you.

Real Help

✞

FIRST	THEN
Romans 3:23	1 Corinthians 12:12-27
Romans 6:23	Romans 12:4-5
Romans 5:8	Colossians 1:18
Romans 10:9	Ephesians 1:22-23
Romans 10:13	Colossians 2:19
Romans 5:1	
Romans 8:1	

UNIVERSAL DONOR

Living this life has been a nightmare from the start.
No father, no money, and a mother with a bad heart.
I constantly have dreams that end with me dead.
It's hard to consider ever getting ahead.

I sit and ponder why this is my lot.
A small voice says, "Consider your heart."
I say to myself, "My heart is fine."
Then the voice says, "One of us is lying,"

Even though its rhythm is good and beats on time,
I am sure your heart pumps blood that's not mine.
You are in dire need of a blood transfusion.
Neither the hospital nor the local blood center can provide the solution.

What you need is the blood of Jesus Christ.
That's the blood that will totally cleanse your life.
It will wipe away the damage of how it all started,
and totally remove the mess that left you brokenhearted.

Did you know that your father was never strong enough to stay?
He refused to accept what I am offering you today.
He made a decision to gamble his future away.
In return, he dealt you a very bad day.

If you do not accept this life saving gift,
you will continue to struggle, fail, and drift.
In your current condition, can you trust it for change?
Keep doing what you are doing, and you will keep getting the same.

There is no situation that my blood cannot change.

God's Answer to Life Struggles

I have conquered every situation that can form in the brain.
Rather you know it or not, I died in your place.
My death paved the way for you to win this life's race.

Accept me now and reset your life.
Let's start to thrive and readjust your sight.
We will target things that will change your future.
Give me your permission. We can't start any sooner.

The offer will stand until I return.
Stop procrastinating. The offer is firm.
Putting this off will not change a thing,
regardless of your decision, you will hear from me.
I already know everyone's decision.
Some will choose life, and others, a death collision.
I know what is good and bad alike.
The bad is really bad, so please get it right.

When you die and have accepted the lie,
always know that my death had the purpose of saving you.
I did try!

Real Help

✝

FIRST	THEN
Romans 3:23	Ezekiel 36:26-27
Romans 6:23	Revelation 1:5
Romans 5:8	Deuteronomy 30:19-20
Romans 10:9	1 John 1:7
Romans 10:13	Revelation 12:11
Romans 5:1	
Romans 8:1	

TRUST

This world was created from the Word of trust.
If you look at it now, it leaves much to discuss.
When God spoke it, He called it good.
Allow me to elucidate; I think I should.

What is seen now is the complete opposite of His intent,
but that should not be a surprise,
due to the acceptance of satan and all his lies.

The very essence of this world has lost its way.
Everything is negotiable, at least that's what our leaders say.
Laws have changed the American way, of disciplining our children,
respecting our elderly, and getting a job to earn an honest day's pay.

Now children are telling parents what to do.
Our elderly are mistreated by the government through financial abuse.
Just forget about getting a real job.
It seems more profitable to steal, cheat, and rob.

It's practically impossible to live safely without trust.
God created the principle to take care of all of us.
This world has decided that trust is overrated.
So, safety is gone. It had to be traded.

Quite often now, new laws are passed,
that destroy the truth to create the bad.
The people who are responsible for enforcing the rules
are the very same ones that criminals use.

Paying them off to stay out of the way,
so crime can go on without any delay.

You know it's bad when the family structure was altered.
Now you can show up with anyone at the altar.

Same-sex marriages, threesomes, and the like,
it doesn't matter the arrangement, now it's all called right.
Black men are being gunned down just to have something to do.
As if their lives are expendable and have no real use.
You would think having a president would help address these truths.

It can be overwhelming, these state of affairs.
What is the answer to these living nightmares?
God has always provided an emblem of hope.
Just look at your money and have faith in that quote.
"In God We Trust" is still the right way,
regardless of push back from those who naysay.
To be perfectly honest, it's your only chance.
Place your trust in God and begin to stand.

Everything that is happening has already been predicted.
The Bible lays it out so all won't be afflicted.
Do you think you were the only one present when that deal was made?
What you did was purchase a master, you silly slave.

The money you accepted that caused many their lives,
will serve as interest on the debt from those lies.
Here is some reality that you may not appreciate.
God was present during every meeting and debate.

Closing the windows and locking the doors did not matter at all.
What you didn't know is that He just walks through walls.
The wind is His ears and oxygen His eyes.
Were you anywhere without those two by your side?

The truth of the matter is you can trust in God.
He is the one who is really in charge.
Nothing happens without His allowance and/or permission.

He is the one that makes all the decisions.

Things do not seem to turn out the right way,
but with incomplete knowledge, how can we say?
Only God possesses the complete picture of what needs to be done.
Since He is love, no need to ponder that one.

Let's stop studying the world and start trusting God.
He is still the Good Shepherd with a staff and a rod.
The world belongs to Him. He promised to finish what He started.
That is the best news for those who are wounded or broken hearted.

Kenneth E. Piper

Real Help
✟

FIRST	THEN
Romans 3:23	Genesis 1:31
Romans 6;23	Psalm 28:7
Romans 5:8	Psalm 62:8
Romans 10:9	Psalm 20:7
Romans 10:13	Isaiah 26:4
Romans 5:1	Psalm 32:10
Romans 8:1	John 20:19,26-27

THE WALKING DEAD

How can man give the definition of life,
when he was created from dust by spiritual light?
The longest day of your existence was the day of your birth.
The countdown was activated the moment you entered earth.

If all you ever do is physically grow,
life will elude you, and of it you will never know.
See, life has little to do with just being a physical being.
All people are physical but some lack spiritual agreeing.

What does it mean to spiritually agree?
How is it possible to relate with what you don't see?
In order to grasp this concept in full,
you have to accept the reality that the wool,
has been pulled over your face,
by satan, in hopes to establish your resting place.

Satan is fallen but quite knowledgeable too.
The purpose of his involvement is always to deceive you.
He already knows that he is the walking dead,
so, his job is to attract all he can to share in that bed.

His process is threefold and this is how it goes.
In most cases, he starts with pride, the very same thing that got him denied.
He places thoughts in your mind that up hold self-sufficiency.
He promotes ideas that lie about your efficiency.

Once you believe that you are better than all,
you will never accept that precious inner call.
Pride always keep you looking only at yourself,
a false sense of security that you do not need any help.

Once pride is firmly established in place,
lust arrives to occupy some space.
Now that you think the world is your playground,
there are no barriers or limits to what's considered sound.

Entitlement is your leader; selfishness is your pearl.
That precious jewel of thought that you own the world.
Why would anyone not want to serve me?
I am their gift and existence key.

That same type of thinking caused satan his life,
while he was in Heaven trying to start a fight.
It resulted in devastation for him of course.
Do you think your plight will be better or worse?

Everything that you just read,
is about the life of the walking dead.
This is a great place to share some good news,
a tried and true antidote for the devil's blues.

See, true life began when death was defeated.
That was accomplished when Jesus rose to be gloriously seated,
at the right hand of God, constantly interceding.
Interceding for those who have chosen to live
forever, based on the work that He did prior to Heaven.

Real life has nothing to do with selfishness or pride.
Those two are poisons that eat away from the inside.
When you accept Jesus Christ as commander in chief,
for you He turns over a brand new leaf.

Suddenly there is a yearning to fulfill your original purpose,
of loving God through being a servant.
You are no longer driven by reckless decisions
that often result in life's collisions.

Now that you are connected to the real life source,
it's funny how the mind just changes its course.
Now looking back, it's hard to digest,
that it was you acting crazy and pounding your chest.

This brand new peace just reveals the devil's lie
that living on edge is appropriate before you die.
He knew the entire time that your death was paid in full.
He was there when Jesus defeated death and disarmed its nasty pull.

Regardless of this, he chose to offer the essence of his core.
That would be lies from all angles, just to deceive even more.
The product of deception can never be life.
Truth is the only way, and Jesus is the light.

So, do not keep walking around knowing you're dead.
When it's all over and everything has been said,
you were enlightened of the facts of being misled.

Jesus will come back to collect His own.
You will look around for help and we'll all be gone.
The devil will smile because he led you astray.
His only mission here was to make you his prey.

Real Help

✟

FIRST	THEN
Romans 3:23	1 John 3:8
Romans 6:23	John 8:44
Romans 5:8	John 10:10
Romans 10:9	James 4:7
Romans 10:13	Revelation 20:1-6
Romans 5:1	John 14:6
Romans 8:1	Ephesians 2:3-6

WORDS

When it comes to the subject
of misery, damage, and pain,
words are very seldom mentioned
as participants, in these life torrential rains.

Weapons, drugs, immorality, and greed,
seem to be the leaders of these concerns.
That's really a smoke screen
to camouflage what's biblically affirmed.

See, words started the dialogue that established the above three.
Actually, words are at the foundation of everything you see.
The truth of the matter resides in the beginning of time.
God used words to create what's seen, and as signs,
for spiritual direction during troubled times.

Words were used to command something from nothing, to appear.
Mix that with faith and watch manifestation hit gear.
The power of words can transform a life,
to peace and love that was once filled with strife.

The minute words are released, they have an intended mission,
to pursue the target of the spoken decision.
Depending on what was said,
they can kill the living or revive the dead.

Death and life are in the power of the tongue.
Examine your words to explain why what's being done.
It's amazing the amount of power words truly carry.
They have been known to stop storms, they're also required to be legally married.

Faith-filled words are raising people from the dead.
They are also the reason that multitudes are being fed.
Words create pictures of reality being formed.
What are you speaking, blessings or storms?

When you constantly said that your child would end up just like his dad,
why are you surprised at the accuracy your words had?
Once that was spoken, those words had a mission,
to accomplish the goal of your son's reciprocal fruition.

See, God has a principle that is also a law.
It was established in heaven to benefit us all.
Laws can never benefit those who are unaware of their existence.
Ignorance causes damage, so God provides assistance.

God says that you can have exactly what you say.
It works every time when applied the correct way.

In the beginning, the Word was God.
Let that soak in and do a brain massage.
He was made flesh to be a living example.
No need to be unsure or have to gamble.

God's word has not lost any of its sting.
It still has authority and power over everything.
God has provided answers to every situation that can arise.
Just say what he says about it and watch it come alive.

He's promised that your belief in His synopsis of the situation,
will completely resolve it, so no need for contemplation.
Words are the bricks that are building your life.
What have you been saying? Does it resemble what's occupying your sight?

Positive words transform darkness into light.
Negative words punch holes in dreams by destroying what's right.
Do you really want everything you say to come true?

If the answer is no, then call a truce.

Recant the damaging words you've said.
Speak with God. He will dismantle that web.
From now on, use God's word for the regeneration of life.
Every word from His mouth will more than suffice.

Always remember, that God's word is His power.
They are there to uphold you and be your strong tower.

Real Help

✟

FIRST	THEN
Romans 3:23	Proverbs 18:21
Romans 6:23	Ephesians 4:29
Romans 5:8	James 1:26
Romans 10:9	James 3:3-6
Romans 10:13	Proverbs 12:18
Romans 5:1	Matthew 12:37
Romans 8:1	Proverbs 6:2

GUIDANCE

This entire world is operated through a series of decisions.
Some have been beneficial, but others have caused collisions.
The greatest of minds have come together,
to ponder the strategies required to so call make things better.

With all the deliberation and time invested,
many problems are worse, and some aren't even contested.
How can so much time be spent,
and the result just barely places a dent,
in all the challenges that drove this intent?

Money and power have both been used,
to give insight a hand, and accomplishment some clues.
Money and power truly have their place,
but they were never designed to address the world's case.

These countries' leaders have forgotten the main man.
When they lost Him, they lost the plan.
See, God created everything for Himself.
His purpose has not changed, regardless of who is at the helm.

This world has decided that information is the key.
God knows that information without contemplation results in eyes that cannot see.
For true guidance to take place, wisdom has to show up.
Since God has been dismissed, just throw your hands up.
You purchased disgust.

God knows the details of every plan.
He can see and hear from the pan handle of Florida to the hills of Arabian sands.
He already knows the outcome of it all.
He was there recording the present before light was called.

He even has the original footage of satan's great fall.

If guidance and direction is what's desired,
ask God your questions. He could never be a liar.
Before the beginning of time,
He drew a picture in His mind.
That picture entered His heart
and love framed its outer parts.

He flashed a small grin, but had to tone it down,
because the essence of His joy began to create thundering sounds.
With excellence the goal, He created all that is seen.
Mankind was supposed to connect with Him in order to glean.

His precious information is protected by the one
who can never be hacked or threatened by a gun.
Real and true direction is reserved for those
who accept Jesus Christ and forsake the world's pros.

If you are really serious about preparing for the future,
allow the Holy Spirit to be your tutor.
His life's course is all you'll ever need,
to handle those who cheat, steal, and lie the entire time they lead.

Preparing His children is a part of His plan,
to successfully rule while operating in His hand.
God is the guidance so keep that in mind.
When you trust humans, you're just wasting your time.

Real Help

✝

FIRST	THEN	
Romans 3:23	Revelation 4:11	Numbers 23:19
Romans 6:23	Psalm 106:35-42	Proverbs 9:10
Romans 5:8	Ezekiel 20:24-25	Isaiah 58:11
Romans 10:9	Isaiah 5:20,23,24	John 16:13
Romans 10:13	Isaiah 46:9-10	Psalm 32:8
Romans 5:1	1 Timothy 6:10	James 1:5-6
Romans 8:1	Mark 8:36	Proverbs 3:5-6

TRUE PROTECTION

There are many companies that are rich today,
by charging enormous fees just to be able to say,
"You're safe from harm, no cause for alarm."

Because protection is of paramount concern,
it seems as though everyone is taking their turn
at being alarmed about the possibility of being harmed.

This world is spending billions trying to protect itself.
There are drones, robots, and secret security measures,
tunnels, firewalls, and hidden strategic schedules.

Our world leaders hire the best muscle that money can buy.
Our government has placed satellites with eyes in the sky.
All of the affluent just move away
and create their own safe place to stay.

They hire their teams and install their systems.
They discuss plans to address all resistance.
Once satisfied, they place full confidence
in what they deem an impenetrable fence.

For everyone else, they do what they can
to shield and protect from the foolishness of man.
Some use alarm systems and others install bars.
Many just wish they could address these horrors.

You would think, with all the death, theft, and destruction,
the message would be clear.
Satan is behind the scenes orchestrating all this fear.

His purpose has not changed. He hasn't adjusted his ploy.

God's Answer to Life Struggles

He still has a mission to steal, kill, and destroy.
Trying to conquer a spirit with physical devices
is like trying to have a party in the middle of a crisis.

Spending all that money on manmade ideas,
will never be able to calm or alleviate these fears.
See, God gave the solution a long time ago.
He's already defeated satan and destroyed his show.

Anything or anyone that's of value to you,
give it or them to God; He will see it through.
He said all is futile without Him in charge.
Unless He protects a city, it's just a mirage.

God can say that because only He knows the truth.
Satan is a spirit just roaming on the loose.
Once he inhabits a body, then havoc is the noose,
used to choke peace from the ones without a clue.

Everything becomes chaotic and people begin to panic.
He is the real reason why things are frantic.
The best news of all is that God is a Spirit too.
The difference being that He controls everything and satan is included in that truth.

Do you want real protection that this world cannot provide?
Only God's protection plan can safely guide—
you around satan and his terrestrial disguise.

So, stop disregarding your only hope of success.
Only God has the desire and ability to clean up this mess.
It is His will to address these concerns,
but He has to be invited to take His turn.

Now you've been informed.
I hope you've learned.
God is waiting. No need to discern.

Real Help

✝

FIRST	THEN	
Romans 3:23	John 10:10	Psalm 27:1
Romans 6:23	1 Peter 5:8	2 Timothy 1:7
Romans 5:8	Ephesians 6:12	Isaiah 43:1
Romans 10:9	Psalm 127:1	
Romans 10:13	Colossians 2:15 (Amplified Version)	
Romans 5:1	Isaiah 41:10	
Romans 8:1	Psalm 46:1	

SENSE KNOWLEDGE

Was the mind created only to be fueled by the senses?
This question seems easy to answer, until truth challenges its defenses.
Living a life strictly based on what one can see, hear, touch, or smell
will lead to a dangerous encounter between you and the gates of hell.

Let's examine the senses one at a time.
Understanding will be the result and fruit of this vine.

Can you really believe everything you see?
You do see my actions, but that is not me.
Your eyes can only see the symptoms of the real problem.
They cannot begin to pinpoint what's really the bother.

See the eyes were never created to diagnose anything.
They were given for visualization to send messages to the brain.
Depending on the condition or posture of the brain,
the eyes are given direction to remain dry or to rain.

The eyes can also dilate or they can constrict,
they can appear happy or they can look sick.
It really depends on the message from the brain.
The mind and brain are actually one in the same.

The ears provide a necessary work.
The last thing you heard, did it help or hurt?
They are there to capture sound.
Without concise information you are bound,
to make decisions that can cause life collisions.

They're also responsible for regulating balance.
Depending on what's heard, that could be a real challenge.

Without the correct diagnosis of the information received,
dizziness and vertigo can be what's achieved.

Touch has always been a way to signal the mind.
Do you remember your thoughts when you were touched the last time?
Touch will send messages that are not always true.
It can be a chief messenger in misleading you.

What about all the times you held hands with your spouse?
The many occasions you hugged each other while lounging around the house?
Did it ever occur, that the hand you were holding and hugs you got,
would end up later costing you a lot?

You married a simpleton. You married a fake.
In your mind, you were sure you chose the right mate.
How can smell and taste lead you wrong?
They both work together to create calm.

What about the time you were playing a game?
You were blind folded and given samples to guess their name.
They were first passed beneath your nose and then to your mouth.
You tasted them all and gave an answer out loud.

When the game was over, you got very sick.
You ended up in the hospital, a victim of a very cruel trick.
Everything you tasted was laced with arsenic.

All of the senses do a necessary work.
They cooperate together to help usurp danger to avoid being hurt.
All of them working together is a really good thing.
The problem comes when the mind is out of sync.

The senses report, but the mind gives insight.
That is why it's crucial to have the mind of Christ.
Now, let's examine the senses once more,
but this time allow truth to keep score.

Now, God uses the eye to see what's not there.
He teaches the ear to hear calm while chaos is everywhere.
The mouth and nose can taste and smell the sweetness of His presence.
Regardless of the circumstances, it all leads to Heaven.

Once He hugs you, touch is forever changed.
He leaves a yearning to be hugged again and again.
A hug much different than between people on earth.
His hug is filled with the same power, whether you're last or first.

As you can see, since knowledge alone can never be relied upon.
The senses require a spiritual mind to properly address what they report on.
Only God knows the true intent of everything He created.
Without His mastery, sense knowledge is outdated.
Get God's perspective. Everything else is grossly overrated.

Real Help

✝

FIRST	THEN
Romans 3:23	2 Corinthians 4:18
Romans 6:23	Hebrews 11:3
Romans 5:8	Romans 12:1-2
Romans 10:9	Psalm 7:9
Romans 10:13	Romans 8:27-37
Romans 5:1	Jeremiah 29:11
Romans 8:1	

It's a Lie

These days don't ever seem to have any good news.
People are hurting each other and acting like fools.
Death, destruction, and devastation are increasing,
all due to ignorance and a steady supply of poor teaching.

People are living their lives according to their senses and emotions.
No wonder we live in so much worry and commotion.
Are all of your decisions made from carnal knowledge alone?
If the answer is yes, then get used to being angry, dejected, misguided, and walked on.

God never intended for that to be your guide.
Jesus died on the cross to provide access to the other side.
The other side means what's happening in the spirit.
It's real and attainable, so no need to fear it.

What is seen
only represents what's really going on behind the scene.
The devil works really hard creating an illusion,
so that he can continue to be the author of confusion.

For example, have you ever wondered why your life got tougher?
Why the moment you confessed Christ you began to suffer?
The devil will fire darts of doubt through your mind.
He wants you to believe that what you see, hear, and feel is actually the bottom line.

As long as he can keep your thoughts and emotions in total agreement,
he can lie and guide you according to his intent.
His primary goal is to get you to question God.
Is the Bible really the truth, or are you being robbed?

Remember that everything he says is a lie.

The reason we die is because of his pie in the sky.
He has never forgotten the fruit of his pride,
how he influenced angels and got them all fired.

His work in the garden of Eden resulted in shame.
Now humans and the earth are suffering in pain.
As formidable as he is, all powerful he is not.
Jesus conquered death, the grave, and the devil all in one lot.

Jesus is aware of every lie he has told.
You don't have to fall privy to his tricks of old.
To counter every move the devil makes on your life,
Study the Bible and allow it to fight.
An example of the devil being on the move
is when you think poverty is the reason you have no shoes.
The truth of the matter is that's a lie.
God will supply all your needs. Don't worry. Don't cry.

What about the time the devil said you would die,
and all the amusement he got while he watched you cry?
That cancer you had, had grown like mad.
The doctors gave up. They were through.
There was nothing more that they could do.
To be totally honest, that part was true.

Just when it seemed that death would be your hostess,
faith called Jesus with the grim prognosis.
Jesus did surgery using spiritual hypnosis.

The cancer dissolved without leaving a trace.
When the doctors reexamined, you should have seen their face.
Satan's occupation is to steal, kill, and destroy.
But Jesus came that you may have joy.

The enemy knows what God can do.
He also knows that serving you lies when you don't know the truth,

is like serving poison disguised as soup.

Being satan's victim is really your choice.
It takes a fool to know the truth but continue entertaining noise.

Real Help

✝

FIRST	THEN
Romans 3:23	John 10:10
Romans 6:23	John 8:44
Romans 5:8	Numbers 23:19
Romans 10:9	Ephesians 6:10-11
Romans 10:13	2 Thessalonians 3:3
Romans 5:1	Isaiah 54:17
Romans 8:1	

SMILE

Misery loves company.
At least that what's been said.
Negativity and misfortune
usually rest in the same bed.

Life's struggles can take their toll,
grinding you down to nothing, a major blow to the soul.
As things begin to worsen, your vision starts to blur.
Your heart rate increases and your mind starts to stir.

Thoughts of demise run rampant through your mind.
Things are rough, out of control this time.
At the brink of unconsciousness, the Holy Spirit speaks,
"Peace be still," as you drop to your knees.

You look up. God gives you a hand.
He helps you back to your feet and says, "In me you can stand."
You start to remember all that's been taught,
by the Holy Spirit, while deep in thought.

Your strength is restored. Your vision is clear.
The crisis is over. The Lord's calming effects appeared.
Life's been a trial for such a long while,
but now you can smile because tribulation is God's style.

He's toughing you up for what's to come.
He knows the future and what has to be done.
Smile because God is setting you up,
to bring Him glory in the midst of the tough stuff.

So, keep doing your best and stick to the plan.
Your reward is assured, but not by man.
The Spirit is working on delivering truth.
He's always present, inside of you.

He sees all you do when others really have no clue.
Just keep going and never give up.
You're blessed. You're favored.
You don't need luck.

Smile this time, even though it's no fun.
The next time you smile will be because you've won.
Smile, smile even though it hurts,
the next time you smile will be because you're first.

Real Help
✞

FIRST	THEN
Romans 3:23	John 16:33
Romans 6:23	2 Corinthians 4:16-18
Romans 5:8	Philippians 4:4-9
Romans 10:9	Psalm 5:11
Romans 10:13	Psalm 32:11
Romans 5:1	Psalm 68:3
Romans 8:1	

SWEET SERENITY

People are turning against one another
at an alarming rate.
Death is all over the news.
It's hard to keep the numbers straight.

Diseases are claiming lives
like there is no tomorrow.
Money is so tight,
even banks have to borrow.

Families are at war,
treating each other like strangers.
The Church has so conformed,
it's no longer considered a world changer.

Love is the most abused word spoken today.
It's wonderful that Jesus rose
because He would turn over in His grave.

With these issues being the tip of the iceberg
regarding challenges of today,
How can you cope? How can you pray?

It's because of these issues
that you can pray.
These problems are no surprise
to those who eat from heaven's tray.
It was written long ago
that all this would take place.
The Bible is being lived out,
right before your face.

There is a sweet calm
right in the middle of this mess,
when you look at God
and He reminds you that you're blessed.

On the battlefield of chaos
and the backdrop of the unknown,
God's peace will safely guide you
from earth to home.

He promises a peace
that this world doesn't understand.
That's why it's imperative,
to get to know this man.

He's that greater force
navigating life's course.
Look up from the earth at God's tablecloth of stars
and realize His might in the midst of these horrors.

Call on Jesus.
Let the Holy Spirit work.
He's all you need
when life is filled with hurt.

There is sweet serenity
knowing God is leading the way.
A serenity that can be counted on
from day to day.

Situations can change and they often do.
Stay close to Jesus and His peace will stay close to you.

Real Help

✠

FIRST	THEN
Romans 3:23	Psalm 27:12
Romans 6:23	Isaiah 41:10
Romans 5:8	Matthew 11:28
Romans 10:9	John 14:27
Romans 10:13	Romans 8:28
Romans 5:1	2 Corinthians 1:3
Romans 8:1	

WALKING ON PRESSURE

We are really going to be late.
Why haven't you arrived yet?
You did not accomplish the task,
that, I'll bet.

Time is running short on the proposal for court.
I need an answer today on whether you can stay.
Demands, requests, and ultimatums alike,
attack from all sides, a mess, a fight.

With a deep breath in and glance above,
calmness soothes your mind,
with confident assurance that everything is fine.

A gentle whisper aptly from within,
reminds you of Him who secured your win.
All disarray clothed in chaos,
feels like pressure to those who are lost.

Walking on pressure is an everyday affair
for those who know God paid their fare.
Pressure's account is paid in full.
Its debt is cancelled because God changed the rules.

Walking on pressure doesn't require your feet.
Just speak to the problem and watch it leak.
As pressure flees and calmness arrives,
realization sets in that He's alive,
very much aware of situations down here.

The instructions were given before problems were born.

Situations unarmed before lives were torn.
Believing that pressure has a rightful place in your life,
is like saying the devil's your friend and God likes strife.

All a lie, because God's design uses pressure as a direction sign
to signal victory at a moment in time.
Knowing that pressure is a servant at your feet,
makes walking on it appropriate at least.

Is pressure increasing?
Is frustration saying, "Hey?"
Pull your relief valve labeled "CONFESSION" as you pray.
It's easy to walk on something that has to obey.
You have dominion.
Be courageous and bold.
Don't save that
for when you're walking on streets of gold.

Do it now. No more delay.
Do it right now. Start today.

Real Help

✠

FIRST	THEN
Romans 3:23	Ephesians 1:7
Romans 6:23	1 Peter 2:24
Romans 5:8	Titus 2:14
Romans 10:9	Mark 11:23
Romans 10:13	
Romans 5:1	
Romans 8:1	

It's On Now

The preacher is teaching. The church is packed.
Everyone is praising God from the front to the back.
Today you feel different about all that is said.
You suddenly realize your life is being read.

How can this be when he doesn't even know me?

I sit there and ponder the accuracy of the information.
I can't take it anymore. I accept the invitation.
I rise to my feet and pray the prayer of salvation.
I have a new life resulting in a new destination.

I leave the church thinking, "Boy am I set!"
Not realizing the battle hasn't even started yet.
Shortly thereafter, satan gets the news.
He has lost another soul that he thought was fooled.

He sends out a command to destroy that man.
All this is happening and you have no clue.
It's on now, the battle between lies and the truth.
As you study the Bible and change what you do,
some start to ridicule and don't want to be around you.

You try to understand why they are no longer a fan.
You thought your new life came without a price.
I don't know why, because it cost Jesus His life.

Why would it not cost you yours,
when emulating Jesus is the primary chore?
Being Jesus meant pain, betrayal, and crucifixion.
When you gave your life, it meant the same depiction.

It's on now. Satan is upset.
He cannot stand the fact that it's Jesus you've met.
There is nothing he can do about you getting to heaven,
but that doesn't stop his daily interference, all seven.

Seven days a week, twenty-four hours a day,
satan is working, tempting you to play.
Why do you think your past has a voice,
always challenging the authenticity of your choice?

Satan is aware that the mind is the key,
to whether you live in bondage or celebrate being free.
Always remember this for rest of your life.
God has the remedy for all of life's strife.

When trouble comes, and believe me it will,
look into your Bible to see how you're sealed.
The Blood of Jesus Christ is protecting your life.
The Holy Spirit is your conductor, controlling everything in sight.

Even when things appear to be out of control,
that's because of fear and your malnourished soul.
Keep praying, studying, and believing in God.
Keep watching as God dissipates that mirage.

Giving your life to Christ started a real war.
How can two antagonists coexist in the same core?
Even though it's on now, these battles are necessary.
Faith requires endurance because it's you it has to carry.

So, accept peace in the midst of your storms.
They are not meant to destroy, but to help you transform.
The goal is the same, regardless of what is going on,
to be like Christ and cause satan's kingdom harm.

It truly is on!

Real Help
✟

FIRST	THEN	
Romans 3:23	Romans 10:14	Ecclesiastes 12:13-14
Romans 6:23	1 Peter 5:8	
Romans 5:8	John 10:10	
Romans 10:9	Ephesians 4:30	
Romans 10:13	John 8:12	
Romans 5:1	Ephesians 5:8	
Romans 8:1	Psalm 27:1	

YOU

When the world seems so big and you appear to be small,
remember that you are the reason that God created it all.
In the beginning, He put it strategically in place.
Then He had a meeting with Himself, face to face,
to discuss the case.

After intense deliberation, the plan was made clear.
Only His image and likeness would suffice down here.
So, He fashioned man and gave them life.
The word them is used because man embodies wife.

He gave them dominion and said to run the show.
You represent me, now obey and go.
God always knew they were housing a foe.
Obedience is not genuine without the option to say "no."

A decision was made that forced a trade.
Authority switched hands and man got banned.
Sin was born and death given life.
Now good and evil will always fight.

God could never be caught off guard.
He knew that man alone could never be in charge.
To set this straight and make it all right,
He sent Jesus to earth to give His life.

What Adam and Eve did, never affected His plan,
for you or I to end up in the promised land.
The promised land today is His heavenly place,
with mansions, gold, and the ambiance of His face.

It's clear how much work God chose to do,
to express the fact that He really loves you.
When He created the world, He created you too.
In His mind, you are the bigger of the two.

Regardless of the situation, God doesn't see you where you are,
but where you're destined to be.
If you stop short of His goal,
you will never be free.

You were created for greatness.
God designed it that way.
How can the greatest produce an offspring named great
and result in mayday?

It's all about you, so keep that in mind
the next time insignificance starts to fuss and whine.
With all that's happened, there's still a chance,
to maximize yourself by following His plan.

You aren't here just because it happened that way.
You were planned and prepared to address a specific case.
You have something special that no one else can provide.
It's all for His glory to seek and save lives.

Every now and then, say in your mind,
"God is my help. I'll be just fine".
Believe it when you say it because you're not lying!

Real Help
✝

FIRST	THEN	
Romans 3:23	Genesis 1:1	Psalm 124:8
Romans 6:23	Genesis 1:26-28	Psalm 121:2
Romans 5:8	Genesis 2:7	
Romans 10:9	Ephesians 2:10	
Romans 10:13	Ephesians 1:4-5	
Romans 5:1	Isaiah 41:10	
Romans 8:1	Hebrews 4:16	

SINASIUM

Before time had numbers,
God had a plan
to build a paradise
made just for man.

When His plan was complete,
He began to speak.
Suddenly everything He said,
He started to see.

Once completely satisfied,
He gave it all to man.
He told him to keep and protect the land.

That did not go anywhere close to His instructions.
Man's disobedience caused major interruptions.
That happened then and hasn't changed today.
We've still not learned the lesson from not listening to what God says!

As God looks down from His heavenly seat,
do you think He's astonished at what He sees?
After all, when He created this place, He called it good,
but free will and disobedience changed that to wood.

This place is on fire and the flames are out of control.
Everything is smoldering because of the lies being told.
Sin is performing on every stage.
Just pull back the curtain and watch the blaze.

There seems to be some confusion about what I'm talking about.

God's Answer to Life Struggles

I have provided some evidence just to help you out.
The major industries that claim the American dream,
are the same ones making deals for the opposing team.

Justice is still right and worthy of trust,
but some got it confused thinking it meant "Just Us."
Laws are being passed that God would never endorse.
You would think that would matter considering He wrote the course.

People are doing anything that comes to mind.
That is very scary because now immorality has no line.
With no line of demarcation, sin is on a permanent staycation.

Watch the news. Read the paper.
Listen to the radio commentator.
There is one group of subjects that connects them all.
It's either crime, greed, or a sexual free-for-all.

Just about every state has a high crime rate.
The price of education has increased as a sign
that inequality is the goal and hatred is still fine.

People are being tricked out of their retirements and trust.
Others are saying, "That's fine, so long as it's not us."
A great many are shooting poison in their veins,
not even caring about the morbid effects on the brain.

Grocery stores, care centers, and churches are being eliminated,
while liquor stores, drug houses, and strip clubs are being celebrated.
If you put too much stake in what's going on,
you would think that God has left His throne.

He is still there and abreast of it all.
He hears the prayers every time saints call.
What's going on now really makes Him frown,
considering He's the owner of this cesspool lounge.

126

He knew it would all happen, so He wasn't caught napping.
Since it has no class, this world will not last.
It has an expiration date.
God has a brand new one to take its place.
And guess what?
It's right on pace.

Once the old has been replaced by the new,
life will be accompanied by only love, justice, and truth.
Every day will be completely filled with awe,
because God's presence is love, and love doesn't need law.

Real Help
✟

FIRST	THEN	
Romans 3:23	Genesis 1:3-4,6,7	1 John 5:15
Romans 6:23	Genesis 1:9-27	John 9:31
Romans 5:8	Ephesians 2:1-3	Psalm 24:1
Romans 10:9	Colossians 2:13-14	Psalm 147:5
Romans 10:13	Galatians 5:16-26	Psalm 121:3-4
Romans 5:1	Isaiah 30:18	Revelation 21:1-4
Romans 8:1	1 Peter 3:1	